AL-KINDI

THE FATHER OF ISLAMIC PHILOSOPHY

PHYSICIANS, SCIENTISTS, AND MATHEMATICIANS

OF THE ISLAMIC WORLD™

AL-KINDI

THE FATHER OF ISLAMIC PHILOSOPHY

BRIDGET LIM
AND JENNIFER VIEGAS

ROSEN PUBLISHING®
New York

Published in 2017 by The Rosen Publishing Group, Inc.
29 East 21st Street, New York, NY 10010

First Edition

Library of Congress Cataloging-in-Publication Data

Names: Lim, Bridget, author. | Viegas, Jennifer, author.
Title: Al-Kindi / Bridget Lim and Jennifer Viegas.
Description: First Edition. | New York : Rosen Publishing, 2017. | Series: Physicians, scientists, and mathematicians of the Islamic world | Includes bibliographical references and index.
Identifiers: LCCN 2015045844 | ISBN 9781508171386 (library bound)
Subjects: LCSH: Kindåi, -approximately 873—Juvenile literature. | Muslim philosophers—Biography—Juvenile literature.
Classification: LCC B753.K54 L56 2016 | DDC 181/.6—dc23
LC record available at http://lccn.loc.gov/2015045844

Manufactured in China

CONTENTS

INTRODUCTION

He is Abu Yousef Yaqub ibn Ishaq al-Kindi, and many scholars believe that he was the Muslim world's first philosopher. To imagine the world he lived in, one must travel back to when ancient Greece culturally dominated the Mediterranean region and surrounding areas.

Most anthropologists today believe that humans originated in Africa and traveled to nearby lands that could support population growth through proper water and food sources. With its water-fed "Fertile Crescent," Mesopotamia, the land that is today the country of Iraq, was one such place. In fact, many historians believe that the biblical Garden of Eden, with its lush foliage and beautiful plants, existed in what is now Iraq.

Greece and its islands formed another place of early human settlement. For thousands of years, before Rome's dominance at around 146 BCE, Greece flourished. Economic and political stability, combined with advanced methods of scholarship and social organization, created a rich environment within ancient Greece that produced numerous philosophers, scientists, and other academics, such as Socrates, Plato, and

Al-Kindi is known as the father of Arab philosophy. This renowned scholar studied ancient Greek philosophy and adapted it for the Islamic world.

Aristotle.The teachings of these men remain influential today. Al-Kindi revered their work and desired to introduce what were called the foreign sciences to the Arabs.

The Arabs, however, had also evolved their own culture. While agriculture likely originated around the Fertile Crescent near central Persia, many surrounding areas were in the desert. An entirely different lifestyle, therefore, evolved in the region, which is today known as the Middle East. Nomadic tribes took their families and animal herds across the desert landscape. This way of living led to certain traditions and spiritual beliefs that mirrored the Arabic way of life. Westerners did not understand many Arab regulations and traditions.

This reticence in the West, combined with the Arabs' own desire to establish a distinctive culture, contributed to the East-West divide. The Arabs did not completely trust views from ancient Greece, Rome, and existing Jewish settlements. This mistrust carried over to the works of the Greek scholars, who were respected in many other parts of the world. Al-Kindi, however, had the wisdom to see through the prejudice on both sides. He took the best of both worlds and united them together in his own writings.

This father of Islamic philosophy studied the Greek works and was able to bridge the gap between the West and the East. That alone would make his work relevant today, but he additionally brought his own unique voice to his writings. Al-Kindi was an Arab, but like the Greek philosophers before him, his work now belongs to the world for all readers to experience and to enjoy.

Al-Kindi possessed an insatiable curiosity and quest for knowledge that allowed virtually all known subjects of his time to fall within his expert capabilities. During his life, al-Kindi wrote between 200 and 270 books and papers. Many of these remain lost, and researchers have not yet translated all of the existing texts into Western languages. Only in recent decades has the majority of his works begun to resurface. These works shed light on al-Kindi's teachings and theories. Al-Kindi tried to reconcile some of the differences that have severed the Eastern and Western countries for millenia.

On one side, there were religious views and ideologies that emerged from the Arabic culture. On the other were somewhat corresponding views linked primarily to the Greeks. Civilization at the time of al-Kindi was in its relative infancy. However, many people continued to search for the "truth" about life, nature, science, and human behavior from any reliable source, no matter its cultural origins. Al-Kindi exemplified this open-mindedness to other cultures, which even today is a very rare quality.

CHAPTER ONE

THE TRIBE OF KINDAH

Any discussion of al-Kindi must begin with his family. The tribe of Kindah dates back to at least 400 CE, and perhaps even well before then, when written records were sparse or nonexistent. A tribe is a social group that can consist of several families and clans that live together, along with their servants and any adopted individuals.

NOMADIC TRIBES

Tribal living was more common in the Middle East and Far East, where communities of related family members tended to stick together in unified groups. In China, for example, some early housing complexes consisted of apartment-like buildings that exclusively housed members of a single family over many generations.

The tribe of Kindah settled in Hadramawt, in Yemen. Today, this area is known as the Manhattan of the desert. This is because of the sixteenth-century mud brick towers that resemble city skyscrapers. The Kindah converted to Islam in the middle of the seventh century.

Given the nomadic life of the Arabs, tribal living made sense. Men, women, and children could contribute to the family unit without necessarily being tied to a certain city or location. The tribe of Kindah originated in the mountains of Hadramawt in Yemen. This area is on the Arabian Peninsula. It is unknown when the first members of Kindah were born, but it must have been close to the first century CE or beforehand, given the tribe's later prominence.

During the fifth and the sixth centuries CE, the tribe of Kindah wielded considerable cultural and political influence. One of the greatest poets of the Arab world before the age of Islam was Amara al-Qais, who was a Kindah tribal member. The tribe also helped to unite all people living on the Arabian Peninsula, chiefly because of the Kindah contribution to language. Members of the Kindah tribe promoted the idea that a single language, Arabic, should be used among all people in the region. While some individuals could speak more than one language, such an ability was rare and translators were not as common then as they are today. Communication and any kind of central organization required the adoption of a single language. Due to the efforts of the Kindah tribe, the Arabs were poised to join it during the sixth century.

THE PROPHET MUHAMMAD

It was during this critical period of unification along the Arabian Peninsula that one of the world's most influential religious leaders was born. The prophet Muhammad came into the world in around 570 CE in the city of Mecca. He, too, was a member of a desert tribe (Quraysh). According to Islam, which is based on the Quran and the teachings of Muhammad, the prophet was drawn to religion in 1610, when, at forty years old, he had a vision while he was meditating in a cave on Mount Hira. According to the Islamic faith, the angel Gabriel, mentioned in the Bible, called upon Muhammad to serve as a prophet and to share God's message to all people. Muhammad began to preach publicly throughout Mecca.

At first, Muhammad adopted some of the teachings and practices of the Jewish and Christian faiths. Over time, however, Jews and Christians criticized the work of Muhammad. They were often hostile toward anyone who followed his teachings. Incensed, Muhammad and his men drove the Jewish residents of Mecca out of the city, according to many historians. Muhammad and his followers then established their own Muslim society, which prayed facing Mecca. Muslims today still follow this practice.

A number of wars ensued between the former Meccan residents and the newly united Muslims. Muhammad was victorious in the end. The Arabs began to accept that he was indeed the prophet of God. The beliefs of Islam spread and served to further unite the Arabs, who were already poised to join Islam's followers due to the efforts of the Kindah tribe. One of Muhammad's companions and chief advisers was, in fact, a member of the famous tribe.

According to the Quran, Muhammad was visited by the archangel Gabriel. He accepted the call to be a prophet. Believers of Islam follow the teachings of Muhammad.

Al-Ashath ibn Qais, like many other prominent Arabs, adopted Islam as his religion and dedicated his life to Muhammad's pursuits. Al-Ashath ibn Qais later became al-Kindi's grandfather, so there is a direct link between al-Kindi and one of the world's most powerful, influential, and renowned prophets and teachers of spiritual and behavioral thought.

THE SACRED QURAN

The revelations from God to Muhammad, through the angel Gabriel, are preserved in a book called the Quran, which is to the Muslims what the Torah and Bible are, respectively, to the Jewish and Christian religions. The Quran is the Muslim sacred text that followers of Islam read and recite in worship. Muslims believe that the revelations to Muhammad began at around 610 CE and ended upon the prophet's death in 632. Believers treasure its words to such an extent that they feel the hard copy of the Quran on Earth is a duplicate of a text that is stored in heaven.

Like the Bible, the Quran, also spelled "Koran," contains spiritual guidance and rules meant to govern everyday life. As a political leader, Muhammad accomplished many lasting deeds during his direct reign. He abolished the worship of idols, as did Christians. At the time, parents also slaughtered unwanted baby girls. Muhammad ended that cruel practice. He also made statements against polygamy, the practice of a person having many spouses at the same time, and he tried to limit instances of divorce. (According to some Islamic scholars, such as Ali Dashti, Muhammad himself had approximately twenty-two wives during his lifetime.)

He dedicated much of his work to promoting peace and nonviolence, except in cases of self-defense or for the empowerment of Islam. He also attempted to help the poor and to limit slavery, which was common in the ancient world. Many of these beliefs are enforced in the Quran, along with instructions concerning daily prayers and teachings that state followers of Islam should be brave, humble, and just.

Like the Bible, it is almost impossible to comprehend the past and present importance of the Quran's influence. It provides the basis for all Islamic education and laws. It is also one of the most widely read books in the world. The Quran put the beliefs of the followers of Islam down on paper. Now, instead of just reading the works of other cultures, the Arabs had their own book to study, to contemplate, and to call their own. Later this text would be shared among Muslims all over the world.

AL-KINDI'S FATHER

Shortly after the Arabs adopted the Quran as their official sacred text, al-Kindi's father, Ishaq ibn al-Sabbah, was born. He lived in the city of Kufah, which was established in Persia in 641. Initially, Kufah was just a camp for soldiers to rest, train, and regroup.

Kufah later evolved into a vibrant urban center with shops and artisans that helped to define the emerging Arabic culture.

Al-Ashath ibn Qais, along with other followers of Muhammad, took his family to Kufah. There his relatives thrived amid the creative hustle and bustle of city life. Already wealthy and powerful due to the imminence of the Kindah tribe, Qais enjoyed a prominent place in society. Eventually Ishaq ibn al-Sabbah was named governor of Kufah. He served under the reigns of two Abbasid caliphs.

ABBASID

The word "Abbasid" refers to a family of rulers that descended from Abbas, who was the uncle of the prophet Muhammad. The Abbasid caliphs, or Abbasid Islamic rulers, were one of the most powerful political dynasties of the Arab world. They seized control of the Muslim Empire in 758 CE, and remained in power until 1258, when a Mongol general named Halagu Khan took over the city of Baghdad.

OPENNESS TO OTHER CULTURES

After Muhammad, people called Islamic leaders caliphs. Caliphs served as both spiritual and political leaders within Muslim society. On September 14, 786, Harun al-Rashid became the fifth caliph of the Abbasid tribal dynasty. Harun al-Rashid was a pivotal leader whose decisions would set the stage for al-Kindi's later work.

A studious man, Harun al-Rashid supported intellectual pursuits, the arts, and the written legacy of the Greek scholars. He brought people to his court that were expert in all related fields. One of these individuals was a scholar named Abul Husayn Muslim ibn al-Hajjaj Qushayri al Nisaburi, or al-Hajjaj. His job was to translate into Arabic a book called *Elements* by the Greek scientist and mathematician Euclid. This translation was the first real step that the Arabs took toward understanding works that Arabs themselves did not write. It was a monumental move by Harun al-Rashid because it suggested that a person could be a follower of Islam, but he also could be interested in writings outside of the Muslim faith. Harun al-Rashid's openness to other

Harun al-Rashid is depicted in this nineteenth-century Italian painting, surrounded by the greatest minds of the East. This fifth caliph prized intellectual pursuits and prioritized the scholarship and advancement of knowledge in the Islamic world.

cultures, such as that of the ancient Greeks, allowed al-Kindi and many other great Arabic scholars to work in relative freedom.

AL-KINDI'S EARLY LIFE

The approximate dates of al-Kindi's birth and death remain unconfirmed, but it is believed that he was born in Kufah in the year 800 CE, approximately ten years before Harun al-Rashid's death. Very little is known about his earliest years, except that he memorized the Quran in its entirety, as most educated young men did. He also studied arithmetic and Arabic grammar and literature. Science and philosophy, however, were his two favorite subjects.

To further his studies, his family sent al-Kindi to Baghdad, which was the home of many scholars. In Baghdad, he was introduced to the written works of the Greeks. He also likely became fluent in Greek and Syrian languages, although information about his language studies has never been confirmed. It is clear, however, that he was able to read the works of Greek scholars, through either his own translations or those of other Arab colleagues. Al-Kindi refers to these texts in many of his own later works. Al-Kindi began work serving as tutor to the son of Caliph Mutasim, whose full name was Ahmad Muhammad al-Mutasim. It was in Baghdad, both literally and figuratively, that al-Kindi found himself in a house of wisdom.

CHAPTER TWO

BAGHDAD'S CENTER FOR LEARNING

The city to which al-Kindi was sent had all of the comforts that people at the time would have relished, such as hospitals, shopping areas, museums, libraries, and places of worship, which Muslims call mosques. Baghdad during the ninth century was referred to as the golden age of Muslim civilization because people from all over the world became aware of all of the Muslim achievements and were drawn to the city. Just as people flock to major cities like New York, Paris, and London for their culture, job opportunities, and other amenities, so did Muslims travel to Baghdad.

THE INFLUENCE OF AL-MAMUN

Due in part to his family connections, including the link to the prophet Muhammad, al-Kindi enjoyed a respected place in Muslim society. He received the best education. Through his own talent and intelligence, he drew the attention of Iraq's elite political leaders and scholars. One of these men was al-Mamun.

Al-Mamun was one of two sons of fifth Abbasid caliph Harun al-Rashid. During his reign, Harun al-Rashid highlighted the importance of culture, Greek intellectual disciplines, and education. When Harun al-Rashid died, a

After the death of his father, al-Rashid, and his brother, al-Amin, al-Mamun became the seventh Abbasid caliph. Al-Mamun reigned from 813 to 833, and during that time he continued his father's legacy of bringing the greatest minds to Baghdad.

struggle for power began between al-Mamun and his brother al-Amin. This kind of power struggle was common throughout most of the world until leadership by birth became less common. British kings and queens, for example, often had to fight with their siblings to gain control over the empire. Sometimes they would even imprison a brother or sister, or banish the individual to another country, just to gain power.

In the case of the fight between al-Mamun and al-Amin, the struggle turned brutal. A mini war ensued, with both men lining up their supporters to do battle. While the details remain undocumented, it is known that al-Amin was defeated and killed by al-Mamun and his men in the year 813.

The rule of al-Mamun, although it began violently, continued the good works of his father. Like Harun al-Rashid, al-Mamun respected men of learning. He continued to provide financial support for educational pursuits, which were favored in his court. Al-Mamun established observatories throughout his empire. These enabled astronomers to use the best equipment of the time. They also could work under the pay, housing, and support of the court.

In the days before printing presses and computers, the written word was revered. Imagine what it would have been like to live in one country but to desire the best books of another country without the benefit of airplanes, the Internet, or other forms of modern technology. During the ninth century, all books and papers had to be memorized and written down from an oral recitation, or physically copied and transported from one place to another. As such, libraries were quite rare.

Al-Mamun established one of the first great libraries of the Arab world. Such libraries had previously existed in ancient Egypt and Greece, but even they were subject to burning by enemy groups. For al-Mamun's library, which likely was one of the best since the famed library of Alexandria, books and papers were collected at great effort from the city of Byzantium. These books were written in languages such as Greek, Latin, and Syriac. They would be of little use to those Arabs who spoke only Arabic. Al-Mamun also wished to further the teachings within these books and to present them in ways that could be relevant to his people. To support these efforts and others, al-Mamun created the House of Wisdom.

Between the eighth and thirteenth centuries, Baghdad was a premier center of learning. This was due in great part to Caliph Harun al-Rashid, who had gathered a panel of scholars, but also to al-Mamun, who formally established the House of Wisdom, Baghdad's intellectual center.

AL-MAMUN'S HOUSE OF WISDOM

Al-Mamun established the Bayt al-Hikmah, which means the "house of wisdom," in Baghdad. Scholars from many different cultures and backgrounds traveled to Baghdad to work or to perform research at this impressive center for learning. Today it would be somewhat comparable to places like Oxford University in England, the Sorbonne in France, or the Ivy League universities in the United States. However, even these impressive universities probably would have paled in comparison to the influence that the House of

Wisdom had for its time. Such centers of learning were relatively rare in the 800s.

Today students rely upon certain classic works for different disciplines. Students of English, for example, usually read the plays and sonnets of Shakespeare. Students of evolutionary science read the books of Charles Darwin. In the ninth century, scholars and students heavily relied upon works by the respected Greek philosophers and scientists, whose works were the focus of study and translation at the House of Wisdom. These Greeks included Socrates, Plato, Aristotle, and Euclid, all of whom exerted great influenced over al-Kindi.

SOCRATES AND THE POWER OF KNOWLEDGE

One of the earliest well-known Greek scholars, Socrates was born around 470 BCE and lived until about 399 BCE. He wrote no books, but he gained fame as a public speaker and teacher. His greatest contributions were his philosophical views. Socrates believed in the power of knowledge. He claimed that virtue itself was knowledge and that men who knew what was right would act accordingly. He put more emphasis on rational thinking than on spiritual views or the ideals of the state. He promoted the idea that people should be able to think and to behave in a free manner, so long as they followed a rational, or reasoned, path.

Although Socrates himself was a deeply religious man who also was a patriot, many people associated with the government and religious orders thought his views were blasphemous. They charged Socrates with corrupting the minds of students against democracy and worshiping gods not approved by the state, and he was sentenced to death. Socrates was forced to drink poison that led to his demise. His execution, however, came after he already had spread his teachings to other influential men such as Plato.

PLATO'S ACADEMY

The distinguished pupil of Socrates, Plato, lived from approximately 427 to 347 BCE. In his early life, he was primarily educated in gymnastics and music, but Plato later became an expert on numerous other disciplines within the arts and sciences. These included mathematics, physics, astronomy, politics, ethics, esthetics, poetry, painting, and sculpture. Plato founded a learning center within Athens called the Academy. Most likely, the Academy served in some part as a model for the House of Wisdom.

The Greek philosopher Plato founded a center of learning called the Academy. This led to the establishment of Athens as an intellectual and cultural capital. Caliph al-Mamun likley was seeking the same status for Baghdad when he established the House of Wisdom.

At the Academy, Plato and other prominent educators taught their students about all major findings in the sciences and philosophy. The Academy made Athens the center for learning in Greece. For his teachings in philosophy, Plato took the ideas of Socrates and developed them a bit further. Plato believed in nominalism, which is the idea of something rather than the material object itself. For example, when a person views another individual, he or she sees the person based on preconceived notions. The idea, or memory, of the person, remains, even when time may lead to changes. For example, you might remember a friend or an event from years ago, even though time since has changed the actual person or the place.

Plato believed that ideas are eternal and unchangeable. He also thought they existed outside of normal reality, meaning that they somehow occupied a plane of existence that transcended what occurs in everyday life. This way of thinking was pivotal in the ancient world because it put emphasis on the importance of the mind and thought, which could both be shaped by education. It moved people toward independence as individuals, instead of just existing as a cog within a state's doctrinal or political machinery. It also influenced religious views because it put more emphasis on thought and prayer as opposed to action and the acquisition of material wealth. Al-Kindi adopted many of Plato's views in his own philosophical writings, but he particularly looked to Aristotle for inspiration.

ARISTOTLE'S LYCEUM

Just as Plato was a student of Socrates, Aristotle was a student of Plato's. Born to a physician father in about 384 BCE, Aristotle admirably followed in his teacher's path. He wound up opening his own school, called the Lyceum, around 335 BCE. Through his teachings and writings, Aristotle hoped to harmonize all human experience. Every subject was of interest to him. He wrote well-known books on astronomy, meteorology, plants, animals, and more.

His philosophical theories were built on those created by Plato. Aristotle shared Plato's belief that ideas are important, but he put more emphasis on the notion that thought can lead to action, or to something more concrete. For example, a person may have the talent to draw. That is possessed in the individual's mind and body. The person can then tap into that talent by using it to produce a work of art. As a result, Aristotle was one of the first philosophers to address the idea of

A student of Plato's Academy, the Greek philosopher Aristotle studied and wrote about a range of subjects, including politics and government, theater and music, and many of the sciences. It is believed that al-Kindi was most influenced by Aristotle.

cause and effect. Everything, he thought, begins with a cause that produces an effect. This basic principle was applied to both everyday activities and to deep religious thought, such as to discussions on how the universe was created.

Al-Kindi must have been fascinated by Aristotle, as he again and again referred to the Greek philosopher's views in his own writings. Just as the work of Socrates affected the work of his student Plato, the work of Aristotle affected the work of al-Kindi. In a way, al-Kindi served as an extension of the great Greek scholars, even though he did not directly study with them and he came from an entirely different background.

EUCLID'S MATHEMATICS

A Greek mathematician who studied under Plato, Euclid taught geometry and founded a school for mathematics. To this day, much about what is known on plane geometry, proportions, properties of numbers, magnitudes, and volume comes from Euclid's early teachings. Many of these were included in his book *Elements*, which Harun al-Rashid so earnestly wanted to have translated into the Arabic language.

Harun al-Rashid and his son al-Mamun knew that their society would benefit if basic skills about math, science, and the liberal arts could be imparted to their people. Profitable business dealings and stable architecture, for example, rely upon these studies. It is no wonder, then, that al-Mamun chose the best and the brightest for his House of Wisdom. The most famous scientists and philosophers within the House of Wisdom were Abu Jafar Muhammad ibn Musa al-Khwarizmi, the Banu Musa brothers, and al-Kindi.

AL-KHWARIZMI'S ALGEBRA

Born in Baghdad around 780 CE, al-Khwarizmi is believed by some historians to have been raised as a Zoroastrian. The Zoroastrianism religion preceded Islam and was founded in the sixth century BCE. Followers believed in the prophet Zoroaster and worshiped a god called Ahura Mazda, who stood for the power of good over evil. Astrology formed a part of Zoroastrian beliefs, and interest in this area remained for al-Khwarizmi, even when he converted to Islam as an adult. In early history, people often linked astrology and astronomy and viewed them as equally valid disciplines.

Muhammad ibn Musa al-Khwarizmi was a celebrated Persian mathematician and astronomer who was a part of the House of Wisdom. One of al-Khwarizmi's best known contributions to the sciences is his work in mathematics; he is widely considered the father of algebra.

At the House of Wisdom, al-Khwarizmi worked on translating Greek texts, primarily on algebra and astronomy, into Arabic. To indicate how important his work was, the word *algebra* basically was invented by al-Khwarizmi, who used the word as part of the title for a book. In his algebra book, he sought to educate people on all the math skills they would need for daily life and work. He wrote in his book *Hisab al-jabr wal-muqabala* that he desired to impart "what is easiest and most useful in arithmetic, such as men constantly require in cases of inheritance, legacies, partition, lawsuits, and trade, and in all their dealings with one another, or where the measuring of lands, the digging of canals, geometrical computations, and other objects of various sorts are concerned." The phrase *al-jabr,* meaning in this case "completion," later evolved into the word *algebra*. He then went on to define basic concepts about algebra, many of which mathematicians still recognize today.

For astronomy, al-Khwarizmi added to existing knowledge about the stars and planets, much of which came from Indian texts. Al-Khwarizmi studied calendars; the position of the sun, moon and the planets; spherical astronomy; astrology; eclipses; and math tables that calculated approximate distances between space objects. In addition to astronomy and algebra, al-Khwarizmi also studied geography. He wrote a paper that was later used for decades in the creation of world maps.

AL-KINDI'S RIVALS: THE BANU MUSA BROTHERS

The Banu Musa brothers were actually three brothers who all worked at the House of Wisdom. They were Jafar Muhammad ibn Musa ibn Shakir, Ahmad ibn Musa ibn Shakir, and al-Hasan ibn Musa ibn Shakir. Their father was a reformed thief named Musa. "Banu Musa" means the "sons of Musa." Not much is known about them individually, except that they lived and worked at around the same time as al-Kindi.

Like al-Khwarizmi, the brothers covered many disciplines. They wrote about geometry, astronomy, math, and mechanics. Perhaps their most famous work, credited to them collectively, was *The Book of the Measurement of Plane and Spherical Figures*. It was later translated into Latin and became the standard by which many readers measured circles, spheres, and cylinders in school and for business purposes. The Banu Musa brothers also contributed important information to the fields of geometry and astronomy. For the latter, they measured the length of the year and determined that it lasted 365 days and six hours, a remarkable finding considering that they did not have the benefit of good telescopes or observation of the earth from space, as scientists do today.

Although the brothers lay claim to many important findings, they are mostly known as al-Kindi's rivals.

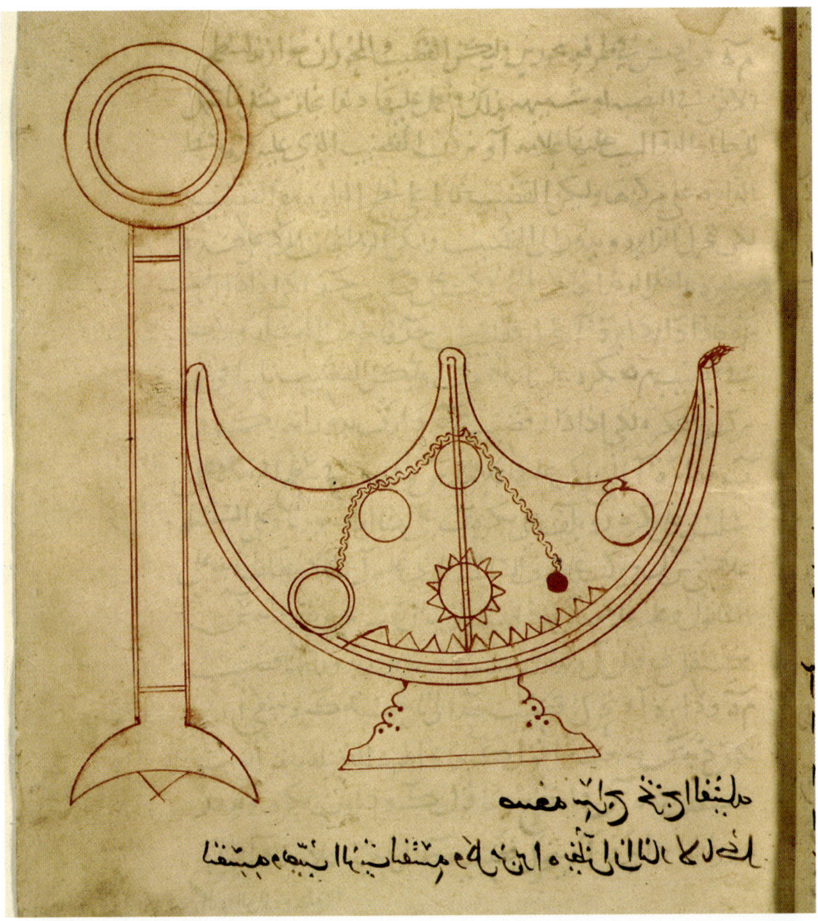

This illustration from al-Kindi's rivals the Banu Musa brothers's *Book of Inventions* shows an Arabic oil lamp with an automated supply mechanism. It is a good illustration of the brothers' work on circles and spheres.

This competitiveness grew over time and came to a head when the House of Wisdom underwent changes due to political transitions.

SHAKEUP IN THE HOUSE OF WISDOM

When al-Mamun died in 833, he was succeeded in power by his brother al-Mutasim, who lived only nine more years. In 842, al-Wathiq came into power. He, in turn, did not live for very long into his rule. In 847, al-Wathiq was succeeded by al-Mutawakkil. During the leadership of al-Wathiq and al-Mutawakkil, members of the House of Wisdom started to compete with each other for political favoritism.

It was well known that the Banu Musa brothers were jealous over al-Kindi's personal library, which he had built up over many years, and his high status within the House of Wisdom. The library was called al-Kindiyah, and it contained several valuable texts. According to some later written histories, the brothers schemed against al-Kindi and conspired with al-Mutawakkil to try to get al-Kindi to leave the House of Wisdom. As a result, according to these histories, al-Kindi was dismissed from the venerable learning center. The al-Kindiyah library was also confiscated.

Over time, al-Kindi's library was restored to him, which according to some historians, occurred through the help of a friend who had to resort to subtle extortion to regain the valuable collection. He was allowed to once again work at the House of Wisdom. However, he lost many privileges within the court at that time, and his reputation was sullied. How and why this occurred remains a mystery. It is only documented that al-Kindi died in 866, somewhat disgraced from his once spotless image. Al-Kindi loved solitude. His death is said to have been very quiet in terms of public reaction. It is likely that his competitors had a hand in affecting his reputation and his later legacy. Thankfully, many of al-Kindi's works have since resurfaced. It now is known just how much he really did contribute to philosophy, alchemy, physics, medicine, cryptanalysis, calligraphy, math, music, geography, astronomy, and seemingly countless other subjects.

CHAPTER THREE

THE FATHER OF ISLAMIC PHILOSOPHY

Although al-Kindi was a devout Muslim who wrote with great respect about his country's political and religious structure, he also had the mind of a philosopher. This means that he continually sought the truth in everything. His attempts to keep an open mind and think outside the conventional gave him rebel status and drew criticism from his more conservative peers.

THEOLOGY'S RELATIONSHIP WITH PHILOSOPHY

Philosophy by nature depends upon earthly observations, logic, and reason. Many scholars of religion counter that revelation and faith are necessary for religious beliefs and theories. Due in part to these differences, many conservative people of the Islamic faith held philosophers like al-Kindi in very low esteem. In fact, philosophers often were attacked, both verbally

Theology was highly respected in al-Kindi's world. Many people did not believe religion could coexist with philosophy.

and physically, because they were considered to be heretics.

During his lifetime, al-Kindi was told that "acquisition of the knowledge of the reality of things is atheism," as quoted in *A History of Muslim Philosophy*. Defending himself, al-Kindi said of such accusers, "They disputed with good men in defense of the untrue position which they had founded and occupied without any merit only to gain power and to trade with religion."

Al-Kindi was a talented wordsmith. He played with the meaning of words to achieve desired definitions. Shakespeare also did this in his writings, and the playwright even invented some words that are still in the English language today. In al-Kindi's paper "On the Definitions of Things and Their Descriptions," the Arab scholar's views about philosophy and religion are clarified with the clever usage of language.

For example, he defined philosophy in six ways. First he pointed out the Greek roots of the word. *Philo* means "friend," and *sophia* means "wisdom," so philosophy is the love of wisdom. He then said philosophy enabled humans to copy divine excellence as much as is possible. He added that philosophy touches upon the meaning of death and the soul. It is, according to al-Kindi, the "science of sciences" and the "wisdom of wisdoms," which allows man to know himself. Finally, he explained that philosophy is the study of essence and causes, in as much as can be learned based on human ability.

The last provision is essential to understanding al-Kindi because no matter how much he supported philosophy and science, he always made clear that these pursuits could never equal the ultimate truth, which he believed was God. Whether it was from personal beliefs or governmental pressure, al-Kindi always made sure that a reverence to God superceded anything that he said or did.

Unlike some of today's fundamentalist leaders, however, al-Kindi believed that a harmonious accord could be found between philosophy, which in his case could also refer to the pursuit of science and logic, and religion. He said that theology was a part of philosophy, and that philosophy and the revelations of God to Muhammad are in agreement with each other. He then added that the pursuit of theology is supported by logic, meaning that, in his view, it was natural for people to question the meaning of life and creation, and to conclude that a supreme creator was responsible for everything in existence.

AL-KINDI'S PROOFS FOR GOD'S EXISTENCE

Al-Kindi wrote many texts about God and creation, but two stand out because they focus primarily on these particular subjects. The treatises are *On First Philosophy* and *On the Unity of God and the Finitude of the Body of the Universe*. In these texts, al-Kindi reveals that he was influenced by some of Aristotle's writings but that he has come to his own unique conclusions rooted in Islamic thought. One conclusion hinged upon his ability to develop several "proofs" that God exists.

There were five proofs in total. The first stated that the universe must have been

This thirteenth-century depiction of Aristotle teaching his students suggests that the Greek philosopher continued to be influential in the Arab world. Al-Kindi was able to infuse Aristotle's works with the ideology of Islam, creating original Muslim philosophy.

created because it is a finite body that has motion, not unlike humans, plants, and animals, all of which seem to have a period of creation followed by an observed end. Anything that is created must have a creator, according to al-Kindi, so there must be a God.

For the second proof, al-Kindi stated that since creation exists as a unified whole, the creator himself must exist as a single force that is indivisible. Here he somewhat deviated from Christian and certain Greek scholars who theorized that holy power could be divided into three parts. For the Christian church, there is the holy trinity. Prior Greek philosophers had also written about how such a sacred being must exist in three forms.

Al-Kindi's third proof argues that a created thing cannot be the cause of itself. If it were, it would have existed before its creation, which is illogical. Here, as in all of the other proofs, al-Kindi shows how his mind works like that of a scientist. The subject matter may have been spiritual in nature, but his arguments were founded upon science-inspired logic and reason. This way of thinking, of basing one finding on a prior conclusion, is still common in science today.

For his fourth proof, al-Kindi said that just as humans know souls exist, it is also possible to know that God exists. He believed that the wisdom in what he thought was a person's soul reflected upon the "wise administration" of God in the material world. The final proof again reveals this optimism because al-Kindi said that the wonders of all creation could not be "purposeless and accidental" because they simply are too profound and great. He believed that everyone could strive for such perfection and that people are inherently good. This love of life, his fellow man, and of creation shines through many of al-Kindi's works.

GOD AS CREATOR

One of the most common phrases associated with al-Kindi's philosophy is *creatio ex nihilo*. This is a Latin phrase that means "creation out of nothing." Al-Kindi believed that God was the only creator of the universe and that he created it out of nothing, meaning that nothing else existed before God's creation. The reason why this idea is so tied to al-Kindi is because it distinguished his views and those of the Arabs from the theories of the Greeks.

Al-Kindi often agreed with Aristotle, but he disagreed when it came to discussing creation. Aristotle viewed God not as a creator but as a force that turned something with potential into reality. Aristotle, who often studied astronomy, saw that the planets and

Al-Kindi built on and moved away from Aristotle's philosophy when it came to creation. Instead of religion, al-Kindi used science to construct his argument. Al-Kindi's "proofs" regarding God as the creator established a philosophy that was compatible with the beliefs of the Islamic religion.

stars appeared to be finite objects. In other words, they were not eternal and infinite. If the creation was not infinite, then the creator may not be either. It is a sign of al-Kindi's open-mindedness that he was able to strongly challenge Aristotle's views on this point, while still respecting other theories of Aristotle's.

What is interesting is that al-Kindi did not rely upon religious dogma to make his argument. He remained ever the scientist. He said that there were four possibilities as to how the universe could have been created. The first possibility is that a thing is nonexistent and that its creator is nonexistent. To believe that, one would have to believe that nothing exists. Moving on, his second possibility is that a thing is nonexistent but its creator is existent. This, too, is impossible, since the creator is revealed in the creation. His third suggestion, that a thing could be existent but could have no creator also was ruled out as illogical, as was his fourth argument that a thing could be existent along with its creator. If both existed simultaneously, where was the instance of creation? To al-Kindi, the matter was purely logical. God exists, he said. According to al-Kindi, God created the world because it made perfect rational sense to someone who saw the world as a great and glorious place.

THE DIVINE, IMMORTAL SOUL

Continuing al-Kindi's optimism is his argument that humans can achieve excellence, nobility, and happiness that all can be of a divine nature. In a way, this mirrors Christian thinking that man was created in God's image, but al-Kindi does not put so much focus on the literal meaning of that belief. Instead, he emphasized the divine qualities of the soul. He described it as "simple, and of a perfect nature." He continued, "Its essence derives from the essence of the Creator, just as sunshine is derived from the sun. It has been explained that the soul is separate from the body and different from it, and that its essence is divine and spiritual in view of the excellence of its nature and its aversion to the passion and irascibility that blight the body," as quoted in *Rasa'il al-Kindi al-falsafiya* (The edition of al-Kindi's philosophical treatises) by M. A. Abu Ridah.

While al-Kindi believed in the oneness of God, he thought that the human soul could be divided into three parts, and that the soul in its entirety was immortal. Plato first proposed the division of the soul into parts. One part is said to be intellectual, another is passionate, while a third is concupiscent, which refers to desire. Plato compared the intellectual part to a charioteer, with the other two helping to drive the chariot.

Al-Kindi did not have much good to say about passion and desire. He felt that they moved man to "commit great sins." He observed that people who retained their calm sense of reason had more control and got into less trouble. As an artistic person, however, al-Kindi did support what he called the "imaginative faculty." It is with this that he shows himself as a unique and groundbreaking philosopher.

No other known Islamic writer and teacher before al-Kindi had ever stated that personal visions associated with imagination and dreams were natural and not the product of some kind of supernatural phenomena. During his time, many people believed that such thoughts somehow existed outside of the person. Al-Kindi stopped short of challenging the visions of the Prophet, however, and instead said that Muhammad's visions represented a truth that no mere mortal could dream up. He did believe that every person was capable of knowing the same truth through the use of his or her imaginative faculties, which seemed to represent his notion of the soul's purity.

Such a theory is again very optimistic because it brings a certain power back to the people. Truth can be found from within, and not just on the orders of another person. Many religions, including Hinduism and Christianity, came to embrace this view as well. It put the emphasis back on the individual. In a way, al-Kindi was more democratic in his thinking than many Western religious and political leaders are today.

The belief also indicates how much importance al-Kindi placed on the arts. If the imaginative faculties were divine, then their material creations must reflect this divinity. Music and art, therefore, were thought to have power and healing properties. One legend about al-Kindi is that he once healed a neighbor's child from a severe illness simply by playing music for the young man.

CHAPTER FOUR

AL-KINDI'S PHILOSOPHY

Al-Kindi's interest in a logical, academic approach to finding truth was not entirely in line with the thought of his day. During the ninth century, there was a growing movement of conservatism that would later become even more restrictive. Many of these conservatives refused to discuss anything having to do with God and deemed the subject heretical. God was the ultimate and the Quran was the holy text, they believed, no need to question.

There was another, more liberal, group called the Mutazilites. These men, while devoutly religious, held the more philosophical view that issues concerning God, creation, and related subjects were open to discussion and to debate. Al-Kindi did not always agree with the Mutazilites, but he did adhere to their view that theology could and should be discussed, even among the devout, including himself. Al-Kindi once wrote that he followed "the way of the logicians," which was likely in reference to the Mutazilites. The Mutazilites opened theology to discussion, which placed an emphasis on logic, or reasoning, as opposed to discourse based solely on faith-based principles.

What is remarkable for readers of al-Kindi today is his consistency. Whether the subject was God or science, he used the same studied, logical methods of discussion. Clearly, he made every effort to quell any personal prejudices in an effort to find what he called the truth. The truth for al-Kindi, while rooted in God, could emerge from any source, even the maligned "foreign sciences" (scholarly works and theories from outside areas, such as Greece and India). Few people before or after al-Kindi managed to uphold such high, consistent standards of scholarship. He applied this same reasoning to philosophical teachings about intellect, knowledge, and sorrows.

AL-KINDI'S MODEL OF INTELLECT

Before al-Kindi, Aristotle had written about the nature of intellect, which he divided into three kinds. Al-Kindi reinterpreted Aristotle's theory and added a fourth kind. It is unclear whether he misread Aristotle's

DISTINGUISHING ACADEMIC SUBJECTS

Although al-Kindi studied many subjects, he believed that each one required its own unique method of study. According to Islamic Philosophy Online, he wrote:

> We ought, however, to aim at what is required for each pursuit, and not pursue probability in the science of mathematics, nor sensation or exemplification in the science of the metaphysical; nor conceptual generalization in the principles of the science of the physical; nor demonstration in rhetoric, nor demonstration in the principles of demonstration. Surely if we observe these conditions the pursuits which are intended will become easy for us but if we disobey this, we will miss the objectives of our pursuits, and the perception of our intended objects will become difficult.

His method must have worked. Al-Kindi was able to analyze information from linguistics, which is the study of languages; physics; math; and metaphysics seemingly at the same time, based on his writing output. He organized his mind and his methods to accommodate the different fields of study. In doing so, he actually helped to define these subjects. Today we take it for granted that schools teach such subjects as math and languages separately. Those separations came from centuries of findings, many of which were derived from al-Kindi's works.

original work, or if he chose to adapt it for his Arabic readers. In any case, al-Kindi's theory remains uniquely his own.

The first kind of intellect, according to al-Kindi, is the intellect that is always in action. It is the part of us that continuously perceives what is going on around us, such as sounds, smells, tangible things, other people, and so on. His second kind of intellect is one that is "potentially in the soul." This refers to someone's ability to act that is not necessarily in use. For example, an artist has the ability to draw even before he realizes this talent on paper. The third intellect serves as a transition from the second to the fourth, which is when the person actually uses his or her mental capabilities to do something, such as draw or to write. In this stage, the mind's potential is realized into something concrete and tangible.

On the Intellect is the first Arabic work of philosophy to incorporate the Greek philosophers' theories of the types of intellect. Al-Kindi believed that the second kind of intellect was an innate intellect of potential, such as the existence of an artist's ability even before she meets that potential by painting.

Note that al-Kindi creates a link between a person's intellect and his or her soul. He believed that life is sacred and not just a means to a heavenly afterlife, although that was important to him. He also believed that a person's actions were important and could influence the actions of others. These views again went against the principles of the traditionalists because al-Kindi emphasized individuals and their connection with God through what he called the "soul," instead of emphasizing submission and group thought. However, he made very clear that the main goal of his philosophy was to know God, whom he and the Muslims call Allah. God, to al-Kindi, was equated with truth.

THE MATERIAL WORLD VS. THE IMAGINED WORLD

Al-Kindi believed that all humans perceive the world in two ways, either through the senses, or through knowledge via the aforementioned intellects. Here he was distinguishing between the material world versus the world that humans can create in their own minds, through dreams or the imagination. Al-Kindi then divided what we perceive into two categories. The first category consists of material objects, or what he called particulars, meaning things that our senses

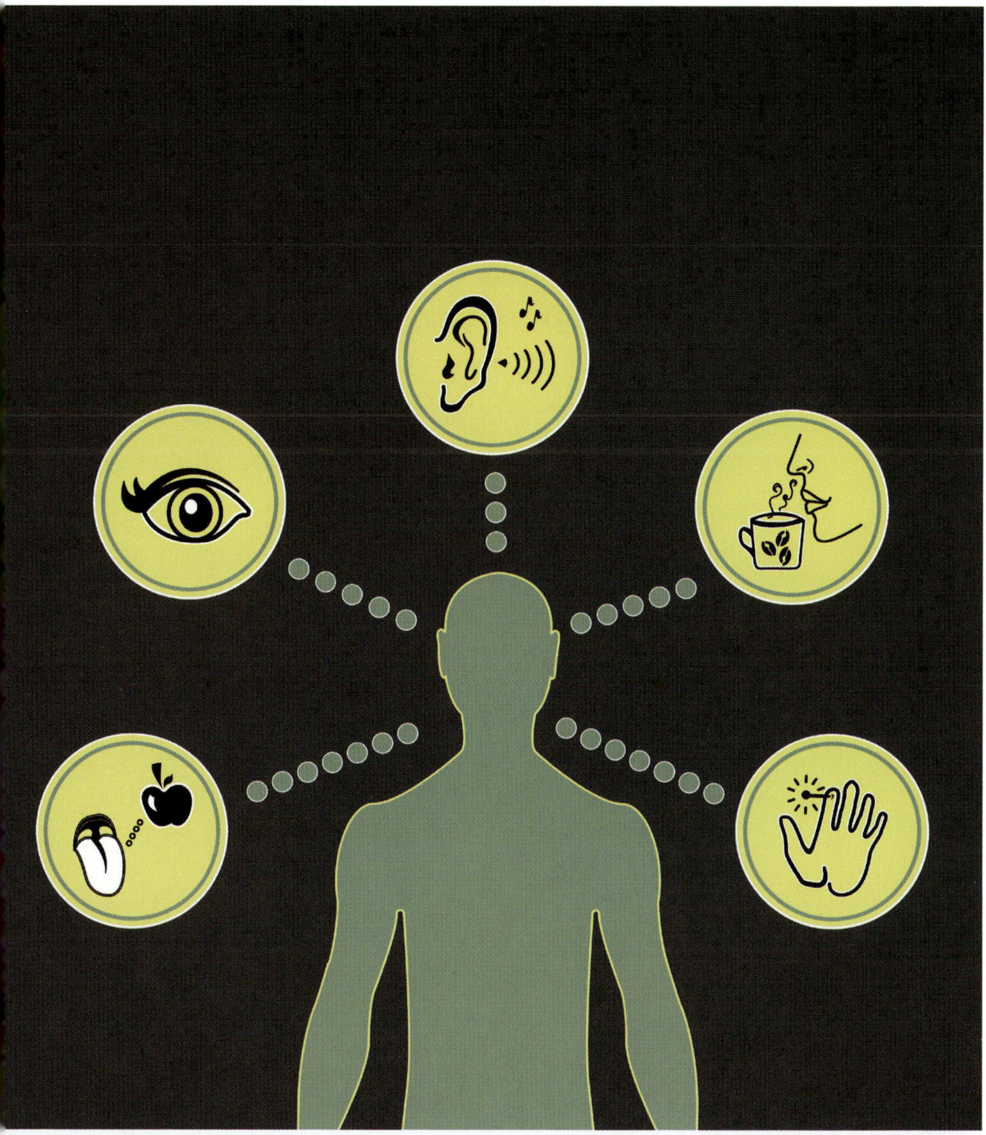

Al-Kindi drew a distinction between the material world and the imagined world. For him, the material world consisted of "particulars" that are picked up by our senses of touch, smell, taste, hearing, and seeing. He believed material perception was inferior to universal perception.

pick up. He then created a category called universals, which refers to the world inhabited by dreams and imagination.

Al-Kindi placed more value on universals and knowledge through the intellect than on particulars. He believed that they were superior to the senses because they could grasp tough, complex issues and problems that everyday experience may not resolve. For example, he often liked to use the so-called law of non-contradiction to turn metaphysical problems into questions of logic.

The law of non-contradiction can be stated as the math equation "either A or B, not A, therefore B." To put this into practice, al-Kindi said things like, "If the universe is a body then either it is infinite in quantity or is quantitatively finite. The universe cannot be quantitatively infinite. Therefore, the universe is quantitatively finite," as quoted on Islamic Philosophy Online. He then concluded that the universe is not eternal, but instead had a distinct beginning and so will have a distinct end.

AL-KINDI ON SORROW

Al-Kindi also taught and wrote on the subject of ethics, which is a philosophical discipline concerning what is

Al-Kindi applied the law of non-contradiction to the universe. According to al-Kindi's philosophy, the universe was created as a finite thing by God. Since the universe is quantitatively finite, it is not eternal. It had a beginning, and therefore it will have an end.

supposed to be good or bad in terms of morality and obligation. Only one of his works on ethics survives in a complete form today. It is called *On the Means to Drive Away Sorrows*. Here, without fear of reprisal from the traditionalists or the government, al-Kindi's own optimistic and clever voice shines through.

He believed that sorrow results from three things: the desire for what is unattainable or difficult to get; anticipating these things that a person would like to own; and then what happens to us when these things are either lost or never obtained. "Things" in this case could refer to material objects or to people. For example, a student could desire a new bicycle or a new relationship with someone. When the object or person becomes lost or is unattainable in the first place, disappointment can result.

To avoid sorrow, al-Kindi advises that we should only place value on things that really matter to us. We should strive to curb our passions in order to maintain what he called a spiritual equilibrium. He places far more value on people, ideas, and religion than he does on material wealth. To illustrate the points, he tells an old tale about the Roman emperor Nero.

Nero coveted a fancy canopy, or tent, to shelter him. Given the importance of such tents in Arab culture at the time, it would be like a mansion today.

Al-Kindi believed that material possessions were unimportant as compared to relationships, ideas, and religion. He suggested that material wealth can only bring on sorrow. If that wealth is never attained, or if it is attained and lost, crippling sorrow is the inevitable result.

When Nero expressed his desire for the object, a philosopher said, "If you should ever lose this canopy, you will never be able to replace it. Great will be your sorrow, for your poverty in front of the impossible will be laid bare." Nero ignored the advice and went to great pains to have the canopy shipped to him by boat. The boat sank and it is said that Nero became so depressed that he died of sorrow. The moral of al-Kindi's story is that we should try to overcome our desire for external possessions.

In yet another lesson, al-Kindi shares a story about the Greek leader Alexander. Shortly before Alexander died, al-Kindi said that he wrote a letter to his mother telling her that should he ever die, she should hold a big party and invite only people who had not experienced grief and sorrow. When Alexander died, his mother sent out invitations with the provision Alexander had mentioned. No one showed up. She then learned that everyone experiences grief and sorrow at some point in their lives. That was the lesson Alexander meant to teach her, and it is the one that al-Kindi shared with his readers.

CHAPTER FIVE

AL-KINDI'S SCIENTIFIC SCHOLARSHIP

While al-Kindi is recognized for his philosophical writings, he also explored many other disciplines. A true scholar, he studied the sciences and became an expert in the fields of mathematics, astronomy, physics, alchemy (the precursor to chemistry), and even medicine. It is difficult for the modern reader to understand how versatile and accomplished an academic al-Kindi was.

MATHEMATICS AND THE MUSLIM SCHOLARS

Al-Kindi wrote numerous books and papers on arithmetic, geometry, and spherics, or the study of circles, which includes analysis of the earth's shape. The titles of these books indicate how well-versed al-Kindi was on math theories from around the world. For example, he wrote *On the Use of Indian Numerals*, and then followed it up with *On Explanation of the Numbers Mentioned by Plato in His Politics*. He also came up with his own theories. Some educators and historians today believe that al-Kindi's work laid down the foundation for modern arithmetic, but others believe that he was outdone by his colleague in the House of Wisdom, al-Khwarizmi.

What is clear is that mathematics as we know it today was largely shaped by the efforts of al-Kindi, al-Khwarizmi, and other Arab and Muslim scholars. The Arabs clarified the concept of zero, which led to entirely new concepts about math. They also developed trigonometry, and al-Khwarizmi founded the study of algebra. Both he and al-Kindi were involved in this important work primarily for practical purposes. They desired better, more efficient ways of measuring plots of land. They were following the Quran, which contains instructions about land inheritance. Calculations derived from algebra and geometry improved their ability to measure at the time, but these fields have had numerous other applications since then, ranging from business, to architecture, to all forms of design.

EARLY ASTRONOMY

The Arabs helped to found the field of astronomy, much as we know it today. Their incentive was very different, however, from what drives most astronomers in the Western world. Instead of just being curious about the stars and planets, they used the movement of celestial bodies to determine fasting periods for the holy month of Ramadan and other important religious events. To create a more accurate system of measurement, Arab scientists improved upon the astrolabe, a compact instrument that astronomers used to determine the position of stars. Later, a tool called the sextant replaced it.

Using astrolabes, scientists like al-Kindi wrote down data that were inserted into astronomical charts and tables. Ruling bodies supported such work, especially because of its religious importance, so they paid to build observatories. Two of the most famous ones in the Middle Ages were at Palmyra and Maragha. At first, these measurements were rather crude and inaccurate. As time went on, however, knowledge passed down from various scientists led to fairly accurate findings on the length of degrees, longitude and latitude, and the relative speeds of light and sound. Arab astronomers even figured out that the earth rotated on its own axis, a theory that was not proven until six hundred years later.

ASTRONOMY AND METEOROLOGY

Al-Kindi wrote at least twenty-three texts on astronomy, a subject that clearly interested him because he mentions the movement of stars and planets in his other works, such as those on metaphysics. In his writings, he tackled such issues as the motion of the moon, projection of sun rays, astrology, the length of days, retrograde motion, stellar rays, the sun, the origin of rain, and other weather-related issues. At the time, weather studies were often linked to astronomy.

PHYSICS AND METAPHYSICS

Physics is the science of matter, energy, and their interactions. Few people in the ancient world thought much about physics, except in terms of metaphysics, which is a division of philosophy that is concerned with the reality of being, God, creation, and related issues. Here again, al-Kindi stands apart from his contemporaries, because he studied matter, motion, and time, the same subjects that challenged great scientists like Albert Einstein many hundreds of years later.

Following al-Kindi's belief that the universe is finite, the Arab scientist believed that motion and time also

Al-Kindi was very passionate about astronomy and astrology, including the patterns of the constellations, such as Sagitarius and Capricorn, shown above. Al-Kindi believed that celestial bodies moved in obedience to God.

are finite. In other words, he predicted that the motion and time connected to any object or event had a definite beginning and end. They therefore could be measured. While tools to make accurate measurements did not even exist in the ninth century, al-Kindi foresaw what would occur centuries later in science, when better clocks and other methods of measurement would be invented. His notion that scientists could quantify most things on earth extended to his highly influential work in medicine.

ALCHEMY

The medieval tradition of alchemy was the science of trying to change metals into gold, attempting to discover a single cure for all disease, and searching for ways of prolonging human life to avoid death. These seemingly unrelated subjects are grouped together under the term "alchemy," a field that no longer really exists today because so many of its goals have been proven impossible by modern science and technology.

Al-Kindi was way ahead of his time in seeing the problems with alchemy. He wrote at least two papers on the subject, "Warning Against the Deceptions of the Alchemists," and "Refutation of the Claim of Those Who Claim the Artificial Fabrication of Gold and Silver."

This diagram from a later Arabic treatise on alchemy illustrates the distillation process. Al-Kindi's work opposing the field of alchemy became the foundation for future Arab scholars. He is also credited as one of the early, if not the first, distillers of alcohol.

Hard as it is to believe today, people in the ancient world, including Cleopatra and the scientists in her court, believed that people could transform base metals, like iron, into gold. The desire was understandable, given the value that gold and silver had then and still do today. From his scientific studies, al-Kindi knew such efforts were impossible.

MEDICINE AND PHARMACOLOGY

No evidence exists that al-Kindi practiced as a physician, but it is possible, given the anecdote about how he supposedly cured a neighbor's son with music and given the many books that he wrote on the subject of medicine. Some of these works are outdated now, but not necessarily due to faults on the part of al-Kindi. He was limited mostly to visual observations of patients and did not have the benefit of microscopes, knowledge of germs, and later findings. He wrote a book on mucus, for example. It was called *Treatise on Diseases Caused by Phlegm*. Anything and everything in his world interested al-Kindi, who had a genuine desire to help his fellow man. In the phlegm book, he analyzes the behavior of afflicted patients with impressive detail. Likely, this degree of attention led to some cure and comfort for the patients who he attempted to help.

Without question, al-Kindi's most important work on medicine was called *De Medicinarum Compositarum Gradibus Investigandis Libellus*, which in Latin signifies the investigation of the strength of compound medicines. The treatise concerns posology, which is a branch of medicine that al-Kindi practically invented that deals with the dosages of drugs. (Before al-Kindi, there was little scientific analysis on this issue.) In the book, he describes all sorts of medicines that physicians and other healers used to cure various ailments at the time. Virtually all of these medicines came from natural botanical sources. That tradition would continue well into the medieval period, with monks and physicians who studied plant medicines, and even to modern times, which have witnessed a revival of interest in natural medicines.

Dosages for such drugs were a guessing game in the ancient world. Today we take such things for granted. When a person swallows an aspirin, for example, the aspirin comes in a certain size and strength. Medicine in al-Kindi's day was more like what is practiced by Chinese herbalists today. They had to measure out natural ingredients to order for every patient.

Medicine was a guessing game during al-Kindi's time. Although it is not known whether or not he practiced medicine in the treating of patients, he made important developments in the dosing of medicine. These calculations are not used today, but his idea to apply formulas to standardize dosage is.

Before al-Kindi, another early scientist named Galen created a method of distributing drugs based upon degrees of intensity. These degrees relied upon qualities, often abstract, such as "warmth and coldness" and "wetness and dryness." If a drug was considered to be "hot," and the patient needed less "warmth," the pharmacist was to add some other ingredient to make the concoction "colder." The system confused many, with the result that drug dosages were never standardized, that is, until al-Kindi.

Using brilliant deduction, al-Kindi applied math calculations to the prior work on degrees of warmth. He created an easy-to-use table that pharmacists could refer to when creating prescriptions. If a drug was to be neither warm nor cold, then it should have one part warm ingredient and one part cold ingredient, which would cancel out any warmth. If the first degree of warmth was desired, the drug mixture should contain two parts warm to one part cold. For the second degree of warmth, four parts of warm were added to one part cold, and so on. By documenting amounts with a formula that anyone could follow, al-Kindi revolutionized medicine. Drugs now could be formulated according to set amounts with the result that all patients would receive standardized dosages.

CHAPTER SIX

AND STILL MORE TALENTS

Incredibly, al-Kindi's accomplishments did not end with his groundbreaking work in the fields of philosophy, religion, and the sciences. He also studied the arts. He was a gifted calligrapher who wrote and copied texts in beautiful type. As a talented musician in his own right, al-Kindi made strides in the discipline of music theory and practice. In addition, he was a code breaker who cracked several mysteries of language.

CALLIGRAPHY: THE WRITTEN WORD

Imagine what life was like in the ninth century. Telephones, televisions, and computers obviously had not been invented yet. Even electricity, which we rely on to provide reliable light in the evenings, was many centuries away from being discovered and used. Music, the arts, and the written word provided most entertainment. As such, all three were highly cherished and viewed as sacred, especially the written word.

Printing presses did not churn out books. Instead, books were painstakingly copied and handwritten, often with special writing styles. Artistic, stylized, or elegant handwriting and lettering is called calligraphy.

Most early cultures practiced calligraphy and supported scribes who copied important texts, which usually were religious works such as the Bible or the Quran. This writing of the Quran was made possible due to the invention of the north Arabic script in northeast Arabia in the fifth century. It spread to the West, where it came into the hands of the Quraysh tribe, which was the aristocratic tribe to which the prophet Muhammad belonged.

Calligraphic styles at the time were considered either to be "dry" or "moist." Similar to the warm/cold/wet descriptions of medicine, these terms referred more to abstract ideas behind the writing. Dry styles tend to be more clear and plain, while wet styles tend to have rounder shapes and more

Calligraphy is decorative, hand-written lettering. Before computers and printing presses, scholarly works were hand written. Arabic calligraphy is beautiful to look at on its own and can function as art, as this example of a calligraphic exerpt from the Quran shows.

artistic flourishes. When al-Kindi re-created Greek works or recorded his own ideas, he used these writing styles. As a result, many of his texts are not only interesting to read, but they also exist as works of art. Arabic writing by its nature has a beautiful, artistic look to it, especially when compared to the more linear forms of most written English. With the flowing motions and deft brushstrokes of famous calligraphers such as al-Kindi, the

Scholarship and other written works were recorded by scribes. Scribes served an important function and thus were accorded a high level of respect. The profession died out when printing became a cheaper and more efficient way to record information.

beauty of the writing takes on a whole new level because it can be appreciated for its appearance as well as its content.

PERFORMING AND STUDYING MUSIC

Al-Kindi wrote eight known texts on music. They were titled "On Harmony," "On the Arrangement of the Tunes Indicating the Nature of the Heavenly Bodies and on the Similarity of Harmony," "Introduction to the Art of Music," "On the Harmony of Sounds," "On the Art of the Composition of Melodies," "On the Art of Poetry" (poetry often was sung), "On the Parts of Knowledge in Music," and "A Short Treatise on the Composition of Tunes and the Making of Lutes."

Al-Kindi played music, developed musical theory, and could even make his own instruments. That would be like a pop singer today generating the mathematical formulas behind the study of music, writing and playing songs, and then building his or her own guitar. Such was the remarkable talent of al-Kindi.

In his works, al-Kindi determined that notes combine to produce harmony. These notes, in turn,

In addition to his many other talents, Al-Kindi was a musical scholar. His writings on music theory were the first in the Islamic world. Along with music theory, al-Kindi also studied music's therapeutic benefits. He is believed to have healed a child with the power of music.

have specific pitches. He said that pitch can determine whether a note is pleasant to the ear. For example, he discovered that notes that are too low or too high because they do not reach the intended pitch are unpleasant. Harmony resulted when notes were combined at just the right pitch and frequency.

Al-Kindi also combined his knowledge of medicine with his music studies. Through observation and sheer educated guesswork, he theorized that sound produces waves in the air. He indicated that these waves hit the eardrum and the vibration of the air movement is what results in sound. Many centuries later, scientists largely proved al-Kindi's theory on sound waves to be correct.

AL-KINDI THE CODEBREAKER

A cryptogram is some form of communication that is conveyed by a secret or a code. It also refers to any figure or representation that has a hidden meaning. The art of breaking these codes and secrets is called cryptanalysis. Today the field mainly deals with issues of international security or protection of high-tech data. During World War I and World War II, codes were also often used when military leaders communicated in secret, just in case the letter or signal was intercepted by the enemy.

In ninth-century Arabia, cryptanalysis primarily referred to deciphering books from other countries. Today's readers take it for granted that most major books from around the world have been translated into familiar languages. Al-Kindi did not have this benefit. In many cases, he had to figure out a written language with little, if any, prior instruction in that tongue.

Today many experts on cryptanalysis credit al-Kindi and the Arabs for starting the field of study. Al-Kindi wrote at least a few manuscripts on the subject, which perhaps were the first of their kind. Portions of them reveal how al-Kindi probably approached a foreign manuscript. He would study the characteristics of letters and determine how frequently they occurred in the text. In a way, this logic was not much different from the manner in which he studied how different pitches can result in harmony. He then would study the length of the overall text to get a full measurement of the occurrence of individual letters.

Next, al-Kindi said it was necessary to create associations between words or letters. He might know some words or phrases in the language, so he would see how these sections fit into the rest of the unknown text. For words that he did not know, he would map out how letters combined with each other in groups of two or three letters. Finally, to prove his point, he took a text consisting of 3,667 letters and broke it down according to his theories. It was in this manner that many of the greatest works of the ancient world were passed down to different cultures and to different generations.

CHAPTER SEVEN

THE MANY CONTRIBUTIONS OF AL-KINDI

Al-Kindi was an accomplished scholar whose open mind was rare for his place and time. While theologians did not encourage philosophical thought, al-Kindi studied and respected ancient Greek philosophers such as Aristotle. When asked to sum up his life's work, al-Kindi always came back to the idea of "truth." Truth is an elusive and complex notion. One person's truth can be another's falsehood. Truth also can be complicated by the times in which we live. Culture and popular beliefs help to form our view of what the truth is. It takes a very rare and extraordinary person to see through such a haze to try to find out what is factual and real, which sometimes can be known only after long periods. Al-Kindi was such an individual.

RECOGNITION OF HIS DIVERSE ACCOMPLISHMENTS

In addition to his modern appeal, al-Kindi received praise from scientists and scholars closer to his own lifetime. A biographical note in the text *Al-Muntakhab* by tenth-century scholar Ibn Qudaamah lavished great praise on al-Kindi and his work. Ibn Qudaamah wrote, "Abu Yusuf Yaqub ibn Isahq al-Kindi was the first to distinguish himself among the Muslims in philosophy and all its branches, and in the exact sciences and every thing connected with them, as well as by his familiarity with the sciences of the Arabs and his excellence in humanities like grammar and poetry, astrology, medicine, various arts and sciences: virtues which are seldom united in a single individual."

He added, "The list of his books exceeds one quire of paper [24 sheets] folded ... He is the first among the Muslims to introduce this form of writing which was later followed by the succeeding [generations of scholars] among the Muslims. During the days of al-Mamun those who acquired name and fame before him were mostly Christians who had adopted in their works the old style of writing."

WHAT WE KNOW ABOUT AL-KINDI THE MAN

The only information about the private life of al-Kindi comes from the writings of later Arab writers. These accounts vary, and it is thought that some men were jealous of al-Kindi, or wished to discredit his work because Islamic fundamentalists did not always accept it. Based on multiple accounts, however, a picture does emerge of his life. He was born into a wealthy, prominent family, so writings that claim that he had a luxurious house and garden were probably true. It was also said that he owned many exotic animals. Given al-Kindi's interest in all things from the natural world, that may have been true.

Most reports describe him as being a very quiet man to the point of being aloof. One anecdote, for example, mentions that he lived near a wealthy merchant. When asked about al-Kindi, this merchant did not even know anything about al-Kindi's work, which would have been recognized by others during his lifetime. It is therefore likely that al-Kindi was a modest, quiet man. But he was also described as having a great sense of humor. That would seem likely, since a lot of wit derives from knowledge, irony, and the ability to entertain, all of which he must have excelled at given his popularity as a teacher and author. Some other accounts mention that he had at least one son. Since he lived to a ripe old age, especially by ninth-century standards, it is likely that al-Kindi had a happy life at home, which was augmented by his success at work.

AL-KINDI'S EFFECT ON THE NEXT GENERATION OF SCHOLARS

As a well-known Persian philosopher, scientist, and even an ophthalmologist who wrote about optics, al-Kindi's writings would have been required reading for generations of Arab students in the decades following his death. Some of these later students became famous scholars of many disciplines in their own right. Al-Kindi inspired the works of such imminent philosophers and scientists as Averroes, Avicenna, and Alhazen. Some historians today think that these men wound up overshadowing al-Kindi. While they may have added or even improved upon some

Avicenna (980–1037 CE) was a great thinker of the Islamic Golden Age. His remarkable scholarship benefited from al-Kindi's achievements before him.

of al-Kindi's ideas, it is important to remember that they had the benefit of the additional technological and philosophical advances that can occur over time. For his particular place in time, al-Kindi stood out as perhaps the greatest thinker and originator of ideas according to many modern historians.

RENEWED RECOGNITION

In the sixteenth century, the Italian physician and mathematician Gerolamo Cardano (1501–1576) wrote that al-Kindi possessed one of the best minds of all known history. During this period, some of al-Kindi's works were also translated into Latin. As a result, many scientists and philosophers from Europe and around the world were introduced to his work.

Al-Kindi threw open the door to Islamic philosophical thought, meaning that he inspired numerous Muslims to think about the Quran and its teachings in a new light that could generate discussion and debate. Because of this, and his remarkable contributions to the arts and the sciences, the twentieth century saw renewed interest in his work. Since the 1940s, efforts have been made to locate, restore, and translate his works for the sake of the public. Perhaps little changes over time, especially the quest for truth, since that is precisely what al-Kindi sought.

A LASTING LEGACY

There is no question that al-Kindi was a devout Muslim of Arabic heritage. He brought his impressive heritage and the legacy of scholarly Arabic thought into his teachings and writings. He also respected the "foreign sciences," meaning the work and theories of the ancient Greeks, the Indians, and the educational output of other societies and races. His work bridged the Arabic Islamic traditions with those of Western scientists and philosophers. Considering the political divide that many people believe now exists between the Middle East and the West, al-Kindi and his work should serve to inspire us all as to what is possible if we only take the time to respect other cultures and how they envision the truth.

Time often makes clear fact from fiction. Prehistoric people believed without a doubt that the earth was flat and that our planet was the center of the universe. The prevailing evidence collected since

Al-Kindi's contributions to scholarship in the Islamic world are innumerable. This father of Arab philosophy opened his mind to adapt ancient Greek philosophy to his own Muslim worldview. He also made great strides in science, medicine, and music.

then, with the benefit of better technologies, is that they were wrong. Al-Kindi was not always right, simply because he lacked such technologies. His views on the origin of certain diseases, like epilepsy, for example, have been disproven, as have some of his findings concerning astronomy. He was often right, however, and his methods were startlingly modern.

Doctors and scientists today marvel at how his thinking mirrors modern logic and scientific experimentation. This passage from his *Treatise on the Efficient Cause of the Flow and Ebb* sounds like it could have been written by a twenty-first–century scientist. "One can also observe by the senses ... how in consequence of extreme cold air changes into water. To do this, one takes a glass bottle, fills it completely with snow, and closes its end carefully. Then one determines its weight by weighing. One places it in a container ... which has previously been weighed. On the surface of the bottle the air changes into water, and appears upon it like the drops on large porous pitchers, so that a considerable amount of water gradually collects inside the container. One then weighs the bottle, the water and the container, and finds their weight greater than previously, which proves the change."

This same use of reason and logic is apparent in al-Kindi's philosophical writings. His conclusions always supported the teachings of Islam, but the methods that he drew upon to reach these conclusions were rooted in science, math, and principles accepted by many other cultures and faiths. It is little wonder that al-Kindi is being rediscovered in the twenty-first century by scholars from around the world because his words often speak a truth that can reach all of us.

TIMELINE

470–399 BCE The life of Socrates.
427–347 BCE The life of Plato.
384–322 BCE The life of Aristotle.
146 BCE Rome conquers Greece, which marks an end to most Greek scholarship from the ancient world.
400 CE Tribe of Kindah becomes known as a powerful, integrated group.
570 The prophet Muhammad is born.
610–632 The prophet Muhammad experiences revelations from the angel Gabriel that lead to the creation of Islam.
632 The death of Muhammad.
641 The city of Kufah is founded.
780 Al-Khwarizmi is born.
786 Al-Rashid comes into power.
circa 800 Al-Kindi is born.
813 The rule of al-Mamun begins.
847 Al-Mutawakkil comes into power and, with the Banu Musa brothers, later persecutes al-Kindi.
866 The death of al-Kindi.
1550 Physician and mathematician Gerolamo Cardano states that al-Kindi was one of the twelve most influential men in the history of the world.
1940s–present Works of al-Kindi's thought to have been previously lost begin to surface.

GLOSSARY

alchemy The science of trying to change metals into gold, attempting to discover a single cure for all disease, and searching for ways of prolonging human life to end death.

astrolabe Ancient instrument used to make astronomical measurements.

caliph A successor to Muhammad as the temporal and spiritual head of Islam.

calligraphy Stylized, artistic handwriting.

creatio ex nihilo A Latin phrase that means "creation out of nothing," usually in reference to how God may have created the universe.

cryptanalysis The study of secret codes in letters, words, or images.

Fertile Crescent A semicircle of fertile land that stretches from part of the Mediterranean to the Persian Gulf; agriculture may have begun there.

harmony The combination of certain musical notes to produce a pleasant sound, such as a chord.

Islam A religious faith that includes belief in God, known as Allah, and a belief that Muhammad was his prophet.

metaphysics A part of philosophy that concerns the nature of reality, often in terms of theological views.

Muslim Someone who follows Islam.

Persia A former empire that used to include parts of what now form southwest Asia.

philosophy All learning aside from technical subjects and the arts.

physics The study of matter, energy, and their interactions.

posology A branch of medicine that al-Kindi practically invented that deals with the dosages of drugs.

Quran The holy book of followers of Islam.

Ramadan Muslim observance that falls on the ninth month of the Islamic calendar, commemorating the revelation of the Quran to Muhammad.

theology The study of religion.

tribe A social group that can consist of several families and clans that live together, along with their servants and any adopted individuals.

FOR MORE INFORMATION

Arab Science and Technology Foundation
P.O. Box 2668
Sharjah, United Arab Emirates
Website: http://www.astf.net
The Arab Science and Technology Foundation is an independent, nonprofit, nongovernmental organization that works regionally and internationally to encourage investment in science and technology.

Center for Islamic Sciences
349-52252 Range Road 215,
Sherwood Park, AB T8E 1B7
Canada
Website: http://www.cis-ca.org
The Center for Islamic Sciences promotes Islamic tradition of learning by establishing institutions of learning (schools, colleges, and research centers) for the promotion of Islamic tradition of learning and scholarship.

Institute of Islamic Studies
McGill University
Morrice Hall, Room 319
3485 McTavish Street
Montreal, QC H3A 0E1
Canada
(514) 398-6077

Website: https://www.mcgill.ca/islamicstudies/institute-islamic-studies
The Institute of Islamic Studies is an academic institute focused on the Islamic religion, history, and culture, as well as on current events in the Muslim world.

Islamic Educational, Scientific, and Cultural Organization (ISESCO)
Avenue des F.A.R, Hay Ryad
P.O. Box 2275
PC Code 10104 - Rabat - Kingdom of Morocco
Website: http://www.isesco.org.ma
ISESCO promotes cultural engagement and coordination in education, science, culture, and communication to highlight the achievements of Islamic culture and support socio-cultural development. The organization works closely with a number of international organizations on dialogue projects, especially the United Nations.

Metropolitan Museum of Art
1000 Fifth Avenue
New York, NY 10028
(212) 535-7710
Website: http://www.metmuseum.org
The Metropolitan Museum of Art features a collection of artifacts related to astronomy and astrology in the medieval Islamic world.

Museum of Science and Technology in Islam
4700 King Abdullah University of Science and Technology
Thuwal 23955-6900
Kingdom of Saudi Arabia
Website: http://museum.kaust.edu.sa
This museum is part of King Abdullah University of Science and Technology. It explores Islamic contributions to science and technology, including many from al-Kindi.

WEBSITES

Because of the changing nature of Internet links, Rosen Publishing has developed an online list of websites related to the subject of this book. This site is updated regularly. Please use this link to access the list:

http://www.rosenlinks.com/PSMI/kindi

FOR FURTHER READING

Adamson, Peter, and Peter E. Pormann. *The Philosophical Works of Al-Kindi.* Oxford, England: Oxford University Press, 2012.

Al-Khalili, Jim. *The House of Wisdom.* New York, NY: Penguin Press, 2011.

Al-Khalili, Jim. *Pathfinders: The Golden Age of Arabic Science.* London, England: Penguin, 2012.

Belting, Hans. *Florence and Baghdad: Renaissance Art and Arab Science.* Cambridge, MA: Harvard University Press, 2011.

Bowen, Richard A., and Iassen Ghiuselev. *Socrates: Greek Philosopher.* Broomall, PA: Mason Crest Publishers, 2014.

Dykes, Benjamin N. *The Forty Chapters of Al-Kindi.* Minneapolis, MN: Cazimi Press, 2011.

Lapidus, Ira M. *A History of Islamic Societies.* New York, NY: Cambridge University Press, 2014.

Nardo, Don. *The Birth of Islam.* Greensboro, NC: Morgan Reynolds Publishing, 2012.

Roscoe, Kelly, and Mick Isle. *Aristotle: The Father of Logic.* New York, NY: Rosen Publishing, 2016.

Ruthven, Malise. *Islam: A Very Short Introduction.* New York, NY: Oxford University Press, 2012.

Scherer, Lauri S. *Islam*. Detroit, MI: Greenhaven Press, 2012.

Sharaf al-Din, Fatimah, and Intilaq Muhammad Ali. *The Amazing Discoveries of Ibn Sina*. Toronto, ON, Canada: Groundwood Books, 2015.

BIBLIOGRAPHY

Atiyeh, George. *Al-Kindi: The Philosopher of the Arabs*. New Delhi, India: Kitab Bhavan, 1994.

Fluegel, Gustav Lebrecht. *Al-Kindi genannt der philosoph der Araber: ein vorbild seiner zeit und seines volkes*. Leipzig, Germany: Brockhaus, 1857.

Fluegel, Gustav Lebrecht. *Al-Kindi, genannt "der Philosoph der Araber": Ein Vorbild seiner Zeit und seines Volkes*. Nendeln, Liechtenstein: Kraus Reprint, 1966.

Ivry, Alfred. *Al-Kindi's Metaphysics*. Albany, NY: State University of New York Press, 1974.

Nouha, Stéphan. *Mathématique et pharmacologie dans l'oeuvre pharmaceutique du médecin-philosophe arabe al-Kindi*. Lille, France: Universite de Lille, 1999.

Razik, Abd Mustafa al-. *Khamsah min alam al-fikr al-Islami: al-Kindi, al-Farabi, al-Mutanabbi, Ibn al-Haytham, Ibn Taymiyah*. Beirut, Lebanon: Dar al-Katib, 1978.

Sharif, M. M. *A History of Muslim Philosophy*. Pakistan: Pakistan Philosophical Congress, 2002.

INDEX

A

B

C

E

F

G

H

I

K

L

M

N

O

ABOUT THE AUTHORS

Bridget Lim has taught history and religion at the high school level. Currently, she is pursuing a PhD in Islamic studies.

Jennifer Viegas is a news reporter for the Discovery Channel, Animal Planet, the Learning Channel, *New Scientist*, and the Australian Broadcasting Corporation. She has authored other educational books for Random House and the Princeton Review.

PHOTO CREDITS

Cover, p. 98 © Art Directors & TRIP/Alamy Stock Photo; cover (background), pp. 3, 20, 61, 73, 94 gfxmart/Shutterstock.com; p. 5 Iqbal Khatri/Moment/Getty Images; pp. 6–7 kickimages/E+/Getty Images; p. 7 (inset) Courtesy Jeff Miller; pp. 12–13 Vladimir Melnik/Shutterstock.com; pp. 16–17 De Agostini Picture Library/Getty Images; pp. 22–23 Mondadori Portfolio/Hulton Fine Art Collection/Getty Images; pp. 26–27 San Diego Museum of Art, USA/Edwin Binney 3rd Collection/Bridgeman Images; pp. 30–31 Print Collector/Hulton Archive/Getty Images; p. 34 Leemage/Universal Images Group/Getty Images; p. 37 Panos Karas/Shutterstock.com; p. 40 SVF2/Universal Images Group/Getty Images; p. 43 bpk, Berlin/Staatsbibliothek zu Berlin, Stiftung Preussicher Kulturbesitz/RuthSchacht/Art Resource, NY; p. 47 Nelson-Atkins Museum of Art, Kansas City, USA/© Leemage/Bridgeman Images; pp. 50–51 Topkapi Palace Museum, Istanbul, Turkey/Bridgeman Images; pp. 54, 77, 88 British Library, London, UK/© British Library Board. All Rights Reserved/ Bridgeman Images; pp. 62–63 Anadolu Agency/Getty Images; p. 65 brookm/ Shutterstock.com; p. 67 British Library/The Art Archive at Art Resource, NY; pp. 69, 75 Institute of Oriental Studies, St. Petersburg, Russia/Bridgeman Images; p. 80 Science Source; pp. 84–85 Werner Forman/Universal Images Group/Getty Images; p. 86 Pictures from History/Bridgeman Images; p. 95 Universal Images Group/ Art Resource, NY; additional cover and interior background patterns and textures javarman/Shutterstock.com, Dragana Jokmanovic/Shutterstock.com; back cover pattern MaryMo/Shutterstock.com.

Designer: Michael Moy; Editor: Christine Poolos;
Photo Researcher: Nicole DiMella